How to Teach Anyone to Read

A Step-by-step Guide

By VERONICA BLADE

FIRST STEP PHONICS™

Crush Publishing, Inc.
P.O. Box 6088
Gardnerville, NV 89460
www.CrushPublishing.com

Introduction

Although the title of this manual is *How to Teach Anyone to Read*, what I really mean is *almost* anyone. Not every student's situation is the same.

Goal of This Manual

My goal here is to create a simple manual that anyone can use to give their students a solid foundation and, hopefully, a love of reading. For that reason, I've left out the fancy language while detailing each teaching step in the simplest way possible.

Rolling Up Your Sleeves

Please remember that anything worthwhile requires effort. The younger your student, the more help the student will need to complete each activity—and the shorter their attention span. I can provide a guide, but you will need to do the heavy lifting.

I've had decades of experience tutoring phonics, stretching back to 1983. I have worked with four-year-olds, teenagers and people in their fifties — all who were unable to read even a three-letter word. Using this method, they quickly learned to read.

Teaching your child to read phonetically doesn't have to be difficult and you don't need an elaborate tome to break it down. You just need to take one babystep at a time. Let me show you...

—Veronica Blade

First Step Phonics Books and Workbooks

to accompany this manual:

Level 0

6 workbooks devoted exclusively to the alphabet. Workbooks 1 through 3 provide worksheets which cover the alphabet sequence, both upper and lowercase. Workbooks 4 through 6 cover letter sounds.

Level 1

25 early-reader books (5 for each short vowel) and 5 workbooks (one for each short vowel) concentrating on only short-vowel three-letter words.

Level 2

25 short-vowel early-reader books and 5 workbooks focusing on consonant blends, beginning with the simplest four-letter words (*back*, *well*, *kiss*) and gradually progressing to more complex consonant blends (*scrimp*, *thrash*, *branch*).

Level 3

5 books and 1 workbook dedicated to words ending with E (*cape*, *lime*, *cute*) to make long vowel sounds.

Level 4

25 books and 5 workbooks concentrating on words with vowel blends (*loud*, *beep*, *paint*).

Available at FirstStepPhonics.com

Part I Phonics Learning Steps

NOTE: Although the teaching steps come first in this manual, I highly recommend you read Part III before beginning this journey, since it contains suggestions for making your lessons more productive. If your student gets stuck or confused on any step, feel free to flip to Part III.

A brief guide to teaching phonics

Tip #1:

Once the student knows the alphabet by heart, begin teaching the names of the letters. For uppercase, the first lesson could look like this:

1. Sing the alphabet and point to each letter as it's said.

2. Practice writing a section of the alphabet in sequence.

3. Play a card game using the letters you're covering (see games in Part II).

4. Draw letters or make them with Play-doh or blocks.

5. Watch a children's video on the letters you're covering.

6. Student completes one page (or only a portion for very young students) from a workbook.

How to Teach

This is a huge subject. Most people go to college and get a degree to learn how to teach. I couldn't possibly tell you everything you need to know in just a few pages. Without training or experience, you'll likely have to learn as you go. But I can give you a few pointers.

Begin by reading the tips in the gray boxes of this chapter to get examples of how a typical lesson might go (a formal lesson plan is included at the end of this manual). I've laid out the steps to teach phonics and, within those steps, often included a script to help you explain each thing to your student. I've also provided tips along the way. Part II of this manual details activities and games. Part III provides suggestions to get through rough spots (or prevent them). Part VI consists of a sample lesson plan, as well as a blank lesson plan.

This manual contains many tools, but I can't anticipate every situation you could encounter. Through trial and error, I have faith that you'll eventually get the hang of this. If you really can't overcome an obstacle, feel free to email us at info@ FirstStepPhonics.com and one of us will do our best to help.

Phonics

Phonics is the method of teaching someone to read and spell based on the system of sounds for a language. If readers learn the sounds for letter combinations, they can then sound out those same combinations in new and unfamiliar words. If they are only memorizing a specific word like mouse, they may not be able to decode OU in other words like snout.

Some Rules are Meant to be Broken

The steps in this manual are only a guideline. I've found great success in following these steps, but all students are not the same. On rare occasions, I have had to veer off the path.

I usually made sure that each step was thoroughly conquered before moving to the next step. That recommendation is noted multiple times in this manual. But, again, not every student is the same. For example, if your student has been working on a problem area too long and that one thing prevents your student from moving to the next step, you may need to jump to the next step early just to keep your student moving. Be sure to return to that problem area and work on it until they know it, while still working on the new step.

Another example would be lack of motivation or inspiration. Steps 1 through 9 could take months and it could take many more hours of work before your student can read their first book. In this case, you could teach the sounds to several common consonants, such as C, R, S, and T. Then teach short A. Knowing the sound to those letters, the student can read a small variety of sentences, such as: The cat sat. The rat sat. The rat sat on the cat. Perhaps being able to read a sentence sooner will give them a sense of accomplishment and inspire them to keep going.

Use Appropriate Materials

Utilizing appropriate materials at each step allows for faster absorption of the letters and sounds, gradually giving the reader the ability, little by little, to conquer more and more complex letter combinations. For the first portion of this manual, I have created books and workbooks to assist you. These products are listed in the beginning of this manual and again at the end.

Tip #2:

If you're well into the sounds of the letters, your lesson could look something like this:

1. Review sounds of G, H, Q, W. Work on any that are still troublesome.

2. Introduce sounds of X, Y, Z.

3. Complete one page from a workbook.

4. Play a game using alphabet cards.

5. Find things in the room or outside with the X, Y, Z sounds.

6. Practice writing letters in sequence.

Sight Words

An internet search will result in multiple ways to explain the meaning of "sight word." This term usually refers to frequently used words often taught by memorization, such as the, to, of, and, a, have, et cetera.

When teaching phonics, students are encouraged to learn the sounds of letter combinations, rather than memorize the entire word. Many of the frequently used words on most sight word lists can be sounded out and are not necessary to memorize. Therefore, I have not included them as sight words since those letter combinations will be covered later in these phonics steps.

In all First Step Phonics products, sight words are words that don't follow phonetic rules and must be memorized. You could tackle them in advance using flash cards or teach them as they are encountered. Either way works.

When reading a sentence or book, advanced words (letter combinations above the student's current level) should be temporarily treated as sight words and memorized until the student gets to that level. For example, some three-letter words are more difficult. The word and contains two consonants in a row which is above the consonant-vowel-consonant level. Words such as cow, for, out or own have vowel sounds other than short vowels and are also above the consonant-vowel-consonant level with short vowels. Therefore, these words would be flagged as sight words.

Ideally, your student would read only books that use minimum sight words to reduce the possibility of encountering more advanced words that might overwhelm them.

The following page contains a list of sight words.

This is a list of small sight words:

a	go	one
all	has	she
an	he	so
any	his	to
are	I	the
as	is	two
be	me	was
do	no	we
eye	of	you

Here is a list of bigger sight words:

been	friend	should
come	give	some
could	have	want
done	move	would
does	said	

Let's get started!

Step 1: The alphabet in full

Tip #1:

Once your student can sing the alphabet straight through without errors, get him or her to start the alphabet in random places and finish the rest of the alphabet.

Tip #2:

Ideally, you would avoid the sounds of the letters for now. If you let them learn this step thoroughly first, learning the sounds of the letters later will be easier.

Tip #3:

Eventually, they should be able to say the alphabet without singing. Ask them questions like, "What comes after C?" or "Which letter comes before F?" and keep doing this with other letters in different sections of the alphabet.

Before you can teach anyone the sounds of the letters, they must know the entire alphabet by heart. There are no secrets to teaching the alphabet sequence. You just roll up your sleeves and go over it again and again.

Singing is an age-old favorite way to memorize the alphabet and has had much success.

NOTE: Steps 1 through 9 are the building blocks to reading and most of your student's time will be spent establishing that foundation. This is the foundation on which everything else depends. The more solid that foundation, the easier the later steps will be. Be prepared to spend many hours on the earlier steps 1 through 9 and much less with each new step. It gets easier, I promise!

Check out the First Step Phonics YouTube channel for phonics and sing-along videos or watch the videos on our website at FirstStepPhonics.com.

A B C D
E F G H
I J K L
M N O P
Q R S T
U V W X
Y Z

Tip #4:

Stay on this step until your student is confident with the names of all the letters and their sequence. On this one, repetition is the best way to learn. Practice, practice, practice.

Tip #5:

Focus on one section of the alphabet at a time, rather than teaching all the letters at once.

Tip #6:

Read part III of this manual to make sure you are making use of all my tips for success.

Step 2: Uppercase letters

Tip #1:

Very young students will tolerate the serious stuff for only so long. I recommend breaking up your lessons with learning games. Read part II of this manual for rules to the following games:

- Student earns points with spelling or role reversal.

- Student builds or forms letters on paper, in clay, blocks, et cetera.

- Play games such as Slap, Concentration or Go Fish.

Tip #2:

Truly knowing the letters in the alphabet means being able to identify them out of sequence.

Once your student can say the alphabet in sequence from beginning to end, the next step is to match the verbal letter to the coordinating written letter. Some teachers prefer starting with lowercase, but uppercase is usually easier since uppercase lacks confusing letters like b, d, p and q. Feel free to start with whichever is more comfortable for you and your student.

When introducing the letters, place the alphabet in front of the student. As you sing the song, point to each letter as you say it. Get your student to do the same.

Both uppercase and lowercase must be learned. However, unless your student is more advanced, do not use the proper terms "uppercase" or "lowercase." Say "big letter" or "small letter" and skip the official words so you don't find yourself spending extra time explaining definitions instead of the names and sounds of letters.

Move to the next step only after they are proficient with this step.

Imagination is invaluable.

You can probably make up games that give your student more awareness of the letters and their names. Or you can purchase phonics games. Anything that focuses their attention on a letter is valid in creating awareness of that letter.

Free printable worksheets to practice writing the letters can be downloaded at FirstStepPhonics.com.

If your student needs more practice with specific letters, feel free to download the page with the writing lines that don't have letters already there.

Tip #3:

When teaching someone to read, it's easy to forget the importance of your student also being able to write the letter. A very workable teaching method is to have the student write the letters over and over again. Since your student may need many hours of practice to easily write the letters well, you can alternate activities by making writing into a game. Call out a letter and have them write it. If they make the letter correctly, they get a point.

Tip #4:

Regardless of the activity, make it your habit to randomly ask, "What's the name of that letter?" Going over it again and again is what it takes to learn.

Tip #5:

No matter what you do while you're teaching your student, make it fun. Make it light. They will absorb much more in a relaxed environment than they will under duress.

Tip #6:

If they confuse J and T, F and T, F and E, etc. (or with lowercase, d and b, p and q, or f and t, et cetera), practice those more. Lowercase d and b are probably the most confusing of all the letters and are mixed up by children most often. Some kids get it quickly, but others take longer. You may need to get clever. For instance, compare the letter to an object with which your student is familiar. Maybe the object and letter have a round bump on the same side or they have another similarity that will help the student remember it.

I have found that if I keep drilling and drilling it, the problem eventually vanishes.

Tip #7:

As with every step in this manual, if your student slows or gets snagged, back up and spend more time on the previous step.

The corresponding First Step Phonics workbook for uppercase letters is ***Level 0, Workbook 1.***

A

B

C

D

E

F

G

H

I

Trace the dotted letter, then write the letter 5 times.

J

K

L

M

N

O

P

Q

R

Need more practice? Download & print this page for free at FirstStepPhonics.com.

S

T

U

V

W

X

Y

Z

Great!

Step 3: Lowercase letters

Tip #1:

For this step, your only purpose is to get your student to recognize lowercase letters.

The next step will be matching uppercase to lowercase.

This is similar to the previous step, except you will apply it to lowercase letters. When introducing a letter's counterpart, you could show them the uppercase A and say something like, "As you know, this is an A." Then move to the lowercase letter. "But this is also an A."

You'll have to explain why there are two forms of one letter. You can say something like, "The big letter is used at the beginning of sentences or in someone's name, and the small letters are used the rest of the time." For now, you don't need to get into other reasons why a letter could be capitalized. You can show them examples from a book, but be careful how long you let them look at the sentences or you could end up explaining more things than you'd like.

Sing the alphabet and have your student point to the matching letter, play games, etc. Don't forget the value of writing. Your student may need many hours of practice to form the lowercase letters well. Free printable worksheets to practice writing the letters can be downloaded at FirstStepPhonics.com. If your student needs more practice with specific letters, feel free to download the page with lines but no letters.

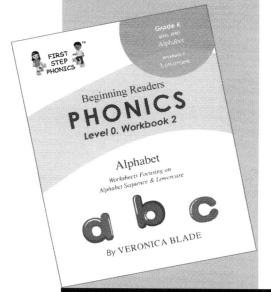

The corresponding First Step Phonics workbook for lowercase letters is **Level 0, Workbook 2.**

14

Trace the dotted letter, then write the letter 5 times.

a

b

c

d

e

f

g

h

i

Need more practice? Download & print this page for free at FirstStepPhonics.com.

15

j

k

i

m

n

o

p

q

r

Need more practice? Download & print this page for free at FirstStepPhonics.com.

Trace the dotted letter, then write the letter 5 times.

s

t

u

v

w

x

y

z

Good job!

Step 4: Matching uppercase to lowercase letters

Notes:

Your student must be able to quickly identify or write a letter's counterpart. You can hold one alphabet card and point at several other letters with your other hand. Ask, "Which of these letters is the same as the one I'm holding?" One of the several letters from which they will choose should be the correct letter.

You can play the games suggested in Part II of this manual, do the worksheets on the next page, or create your own worksheets and games. If you have alphabet cards, you can mix them up and have your student pair up the lowercase to uppercase letter. Also, writing the uppercase and lowercase letters together, over and over again, helps cement this in their minds. The practice worksheets for letter writing can be downloaded for free at FirstStepPhonics.com.

Stay on this step and until your student can quickly match any uppercase letter to its lowercase counterpart.

For this step, use First Step Phonics
Level 0, Workbook 3.

a	C	h	M
b	G	i	H
c	A	j	K
d	F	k	I
e	D	l	J
f	B	m	L
g	E		

n	S	u	X
o	R	v	Z
p	Q	w	U
q	N	x	Y
r	O	y	V
s	T	z	W
t	P		

A a   A a   A a

B b   B b   B b

C c   C c   C c

D d   D d   D d

E e   E e   E e

F f   F f   F f

G g   G g   G g

H h   H h   H h

I i   I i   I i

Step 5: Sounds of consonants

Fortunately, most consonant sounds are similar to their names, which makes them easier to figure out. For this reason, I recommend starting with B, D, F, J, K, L, M, N, P, Q, R, S, T, V, X, Z since they can be learned quickly.

Rather than providing the sounds for the above, ask your student questions to coax them into thinking. You can show them the letter B and ask, "Can you tell me the sound to this letter?" They will probably guess correctly (or close). If they don't, you can say, "It sounds almost like its name." If they get it correct, you can say, "Great! Can you tell me a word that begins with that sound?" They will likely need help with this.

Example: Say the sound of the letter B then point to something around the room or outside that starts with the B sound. Say the word again, emphasizing the B sound. Continue the same way with other things in the area. "B as in box." "B, bag." "B, bed." "B, bush." "B, bee." Do some activities from Part II of this manual, then teach the next letter the same way: "D, dog." "D, dad." "D, desk." "D, dress." "D, dish." Teach the sound, show examples, do activities in Part II, fill out pages from a workbook, practice writing letters, et cetera. Repeat this process with each letter sound (skip C, G, H, W, and Y for now).

Once your student has the above sounds confidently, move on to the more difficult letters. For these, you must tell them the sound, rather than let them figure it out.

Since the names of C and G are soft sounds, you may get the urge to teach those sounds first. But don't. In many cases, the soft sounds are used when followed by an E, as in huge, page, George, cent, cell, peace and those combinations are above your student's level. Be sure to teach the hard sound to C as in cat, can or cap. Teach the hard G sound as in gas, gap or goat.

Tip #1:

Q should be taught as only the K sound. Many people teach the Q sound as KW, but KW is actually a blend of two sounds, K and W. For instance, in the word *quit*, Q is making the K sound and U is making the W sound. U makes the W sound in other words too, such as in *guar*, *suave*, *guava*, *penguin*.
If your student learns the Q sound as KW, they will always want to add the extra W sound and someday in the future they will try to pronounce words such as *qat* and *Qatar* as KWAT and KWATAR. The student will also have difficulty decoding words with Q followed by a silent U, such as torque, liquor, unique, opaque, mosque, basque, et cetera. And if they don't know that the letter U can make the W

sound, they may one day have difficulty figuring out how to decode words like *guar, suave, guava, penguin.* Teach the Q sound as the K sound and leave the additional U sound for the next level.

Tip #2:

Teach the sound of the consonants as only the sound of that letter. For instance, most people pronounce the sound of B as BUH. But if the student learns B as BUH, later when they try to blend the letter B with other sounds, for instance with A and T, they will likely try to pronounce the word *bat* as *buh-at.* You want to distill the B sound to just that sound and not follow it with any *uh* sound. Teach all the consonants this same way.

Tip #3:

Some consonants are made using your voice

Then move on to H, W, and Y. You'll likely have to drill these last five letters a bit more since they don't sound like their names. Repetition is the only way.

Alternate sequence: Another option would be to follow the corresponding First Step Phonics workbooks, which address one section of the alphabet at a time. Level 0 Workbook 4 covers the sounds of A through I. Workbook 5 concentrates on the sounds for J through R. Workbook 6 focuses on the sounds for S through Z. If you prefer to stay true to the above steps, you could bounce around the workbooks and do the worksheets in a different sequence. When teaching the sounds of the letters, take the path that makes you feel more comfortable or seems easier for you and your student.

(vocal chords vibrating), such as the sounds to L or M. Others do not require voice (meaning you whisper it), as with the sounds of H or P. It may seem like you're using your voice for the P in pit, but you are not. The voice you hear is for the vowel following the P. If you were to use your voice for P, it would become a B. Two different consonants often have the same movement of the mouth

or tongue with the only difference being the voice. Examples of other letters like this are K and G, D and T, F and V, S and Z. Your student being aware of voice vs. no voice will make Step 17 go smoother.

Tip #4:

Vowels are tricky since few words exist that begin with the true short vowel sounds. Words like *apron, ape* or *acorn* may begin with an A but

*The corresponding First Step Phonics workbooks for vowel and consonant sounds are **Level 0, Workbooks 4 through 6.***

but they do not have the short A sound. For E, stick to words like *elbow*, *envelop* or *elf* that have the short E sound, rather than words like *ear* with the long E sound. Be careful to avoid words like *orange* for O, which do not have the short O sound either. Introducing additional sounds to any letters (especially for vowels which can be difficult to learn) should be done later, after the new reader has a solid foundation of the basic sounds.

Tip #5:

Some of the games in Part II of this manual can be used on this step. For instance, with spelling, you would say the sound and they write the letter. On the game of Slap, you call out the letter sound and they hit the matching card. During other activities, occasionally ask them the sound of that letter.

Step 6: Sound of short A

Tip #1:

You want your student to begin with one sound for A and that is the short A sound. Using words with other sounds, such as *amazing*, *ape*, *ball*, *late*, et cetera. can be extremely confusing at this stage.

Tip #2:

When saying the short A word, drag out the vowel sound so they can hear it. Get them to repeat it.

Tip #3:

Focus on only short A for this step. Once they've got the short A sound down fairly well, move to Step 7 while you continue working on short A. (We will add other short vowel sounds on Step 9.)

Begin this step by giving your student examples of words with the short A sound. These short A words don't have to begin with A. The word only needs to be simple and clearly contain the short A sound, like can or sat. You can use the short A example words on Step 9 of this manual.

If you have already worked on the short A sound before this step, ask if they remember. If they don't know, you can say something like, "The sound to A is…" Drag out the sound or they may not be able to hear it. Give them examples of words with the short A sound. Whether the word has the sound in the beginning of the word or the middle, drag out the vowel. Get your student to repeat the sounds. All activities in Part II apply here.

To keep the First Step Phonics Level 0 workbooks simple, the sounds of the letters are divided into three workbooks. Workbook 4 covers the sounds to A-I, workbook 5 covers J-R and workbook 6 covers S-Z. If you used First Step Phonics workbooks to teach the sounds of the letters, your student has already worked on all five short vowels. But more often than not, the student needs more practice with each vowel. If your student completed First Step Phonics Level 0 workbooks 4-6, they have already worked on the sound to short A, so this step for short A would be a review. However, you will probably find that your student needs more practice to solidly get the short A sound.

Step 7: Blending vowel-consonant

Short version:

When teaching how to blend a vowel and a consonant, you could begin with a consonant followed by a vowel. But I always addressed vowel-consonant combinations first. Either way will work, so long as you are able to drag out the first sound. On this step, we are doing vowel-consonant combinations. To teach them how to combine both sounds, say A-A-A-A and then without pausing, say the B sound. Keep doing it over and over until they have that light-bulb moment.

Expanded version:

Draw an A on a piece of paper and then a B next to it. Point to the A and say the sound. While still saying the A sound, start moving your finger to the B (still saying the A sound) and then once you're on the letter B, switch to the B sound.

A-A-A→B

Or you can use alphabet cards. Say the A sound while moving the A card slowly toward the B card (keep saying the A sound). When the cards finally touch, switch to saying the B sound.

Try giving your student a word ending in the sound of AB, such as cab, dab, gab, lab, nab. Stretch out the last two sounds, so your student can hear that they are the same as the two letters you're working on.

Tip #1:
Make sure your student does exactly what you do. If you're the only one talking and blending, it will take your student longer to have that light-bulb moment. Get them to keep trying until they can do it.

Notes:

Your student can practice this step by writing it or using alphabet cards, over and over again. Gradually say the sounds faster and faster until the student gets how to blend the two sounds.

Then do the same thing with another vowel-consonant combination, such as A and G. Keep blending other combinations the same way until your student has that light-bulb moment on what blending two sounds is all about.

Vowel-consonant blends

Note that I am not including vowel-consonant blends, such as AR, AY, or AW because they make vowel sounds other than short A:

a-b	a-n
a-d	a-p
a-f	a-s
a-g	a-t
a-l	a-x
a-m	

Step 8: Blending consonant-vowel

Repeat Step 7, except this time, you are starting with the consonant, followed by short A. It's always easier to show the student how blending works by dragging out the first sound then slowly adding the second sound. Dragging out some consonants is easier than others, so I suggest beginning this step with consonants F, H, L, M, N, R, S, V, W and Z. After your student gets the hang of it, then work on the other consonants.

Consonant-vowel blends for short A

b-a	n-a
c-a	p-a
d-a	r-a
f-a	s-a
g-a	t-a
h-a	v-a
j-a	w-a
k-a	y-a
l-a	z-a
m-a	

Notes:

Step 9: Blending consonant-vowel-consonant

Tip #1:

The idea is for your student to feel accomplished, not frustrated. If your student tries to read a book too soon, he may become discouraged or confused. Keeping in mind tips #2 through 6 below, get your student to practice three-letter words with spelling, alphabet cards, games or workbooks.

Tip #2:

Your student must master words and sentences before tackling an entire book. Without adequate practice with the first two, attempting to read an entire book can be overwhelming, no matter how simple the book. Workbooks are a great way to provide practice and bridge the gap between sounding out one word and completing their first book.

Finally, your student is ready to read actual words. Begin this step by having your student blend the same way as the two previous steps. Except this time, you're adding an extra letter. Begin with a consonant, such as B. Add A, then add another letter, such as D. Say the first sound then, without pausing, add the second sound and finally the third sound. Point to each letter as you make each sound. Repeat. Get your student to do it too.

Three-letter short A words:

bat	gas	pal	tap
bag	jam	pan	van
cab	mad	pat	wag
cap	man	rag	wax
can	map	ran	yam
cat	mat	rat	yap
dad	nab	sad	zap
fan	nag	sat	
fat	nap	tag	
gal	pad	tan	

Reminder: Alternate reading with activities, such as workbooks, alphabet cards, spelling, and games mentioned in Part II of this manual.

The following several pages contain a list of words for the remaining short vowels to prepare your student for sentences and, eventually, books.

Here is a list of simple short E words:

Ed	hen	Meg	vex
bed	hex	ref	web
beg	jet	rep	wed
bet	keg	rev	wet
den	led	set	yep
fed	leg	ten	
get	let	vet	

Tip #3:
Once your student can read sentences fairly easily, he or she can tackle reading a book. Find books that stick to three-letter words using short vowels, ideally one short vowel at a time. Avoid books that slip in bigger words, quotation marks, exclamation points, question marks, et cetera, or anything else above this reading level.

Tip #4:
Keep it simple and let them thoroughly absorb three-letter words with short A before moving onto another vowel.

Tip #5:
Very likely, your student will need to read several three-letter word books focusing on short A before mastering that vowel. They may even need to do workbooks before graduating to something else.

Tip #6:

When your student has mastered short A, you could work on short E next, but keep in mind that teaching short I immediately after short E can be confusing since short E and short I sound very similar. Although the sample short-vowel words are listed in A, E, I, O, U sequence, I recommend beginning with short A, and then working on short E next, but skipping short I and leaving it for last. Regardless which sequence you decide to teach the short vowels, if your student doesn't practice each one enough, the next vowel—and possibly all of them—can become extremely confusing.

Here is a list of simple short I words:

if	fit	mix	sit
in	fix	nip	six
it	gig	nix	tin
bid	hid	pig	tip
big	him	pin	wig
bin	hip	pit	win
bit	his	rid	wit
did	hit	rib	yip
dim	jig	rig	zig
din	kid	rim	zip
dip	kit	rip	zit
fib	lid	sin	
fig	lip	sip	
fin	lit	sis	

Here is a list of simple short O words:

Notes:

on	don	lob	pot
ox	dot	log	pox
bob	fog	lop	rob
bog	fox	lot	rod
bop	gob	lox	rot
box	god	mob	sob
cob	got	mod	son
cod	hog	mom	sop
cog	hop	mop	top
con	hot	nod	tot
cop	job	not	yon
cot	jog	pod	
dog	jot	pop	

Tip #7:

Students tend to memorize words they see often. Just because they can now read a word doesn't mean that they truly know the sounds and will be able to read an unfamiliar word. To make sure they know the sounds and will be able to read any short-vowel three-letter word, the final test for all of the substeps in Step 9 would be giving your student made-up words. If your student can easily sound out nonword letter combinations that they've never seen before, such as K-O-D, Z-U-M, V-I-B, D-A-X, H-E-J, et cetera, and they've had plenty of practice reading books with three-letter words, you can safely give them a pass and move to the next step.

Here is a list of simple short U words:

up	dud	mud	rum
us	dug	mug	run
bud	fun	mum	rut
bug	gum	nub	sub
bum	gun	nun	sum
bun	gut	nut	sun
bus	hub	pub	sup
but	hug	pug	tub
cub	hum	pun	tug
cud	hut	pup	tux
cup	jug	pus	yum
cut	jut	rub	
dub	lug	rug	

The corresponding First Step Phonics workbooks for this step are the five **Level 1 Workbooks: A, E, I, O, U** *(one workbook for each short vowel).*
Level 1 also has early-reader books (five full-color books for each short vowel) utilizing only three-letter words.

Step 10: Consonant blends

Many early-reader books have introduced vowel blends by now with words like **mouse** or **street**. Avoid vowel blends for now and focus on only short vowels and consonant blends. But start small. A great way to gently ease them into an extra consonant sound is by adding an additional consonant at the end of the word while maintaining only three sounds. The words are four letters (or three in some cases below) but the sounds are still consonant-vowel-consonant (or vowel-consonant). Here are examples of these words:

CK	back, buck, duck, deck, dock, hack, heck, hock, jock, kick, lick, lock, luck, lack, mock, muck, nick, neck, puck, pack, pick, peck, rock, rack, sack, sick, suck, sock, tack, tick, tock, tuck, wick, yuck
DD	add, odd
FF	buff, cuff, huff, muff, off, puff
GG	egg
LL	ill, bell, bill, dill, doll, fill, fell, gill, hell, hill, kill, mill, pill, sell, sill, till, tell, well, will, yell
NN	Ann
SS	bass, boss, cuss, fuss, hiss, kiss, lass, less, loss, mass, mess, miss, moss, muss, pass, sass, toss
TT	butt, mutt
ZZ	buzz, fizz, jazz, razz

*The corresponding First Step Phonics books for this step are **Level 2, Set 1**. Workbook is **Level 2, Workbook 1**.*

Tip #1:
Make sure your student does exactly what you do. If you're the only one talking and blending, it will take your student longer to have that light-bulb moment. Get them to keep trying until they can do it.

33

Notes:

The next step would be to go over words that end with two consonant sounds. We tackle the two sounds at the *end* of words first because most students find it easier to add a sound at the end of a word than at the beginning. Get them used to words like these:

CT	act, duct, fact
FT	aft, daft, heft, left, lift, loft, rift, sift, soft, tuft
LD	held, meld
LF	elf, golf
LK	bulk, sulk, milk, silk
LP	gulp, help, kelp, pulp, yelp
LT	belt, felt, hilt, kilt, lilt, melt, pelt, tilt, welt
MP	amp, bump, camp, damp, dump, gimp, hump, jump, lamp, limp, lump, pump, ramp, romp, rump
ND	and, band, bend, bond, end, fend, fond, hand, land, lend, mend, pond, sand, send, tend, wind
NG	ding, dung, gong, hung, king, long, lung, ping, pong, ring, rung, sing, song, sung, tong, wing, zing
NK	bonk, bunk, conk, dunk, funk, gunk, honk, hunk, ink, junk, kink, link, mink, pink, punk, rink, sunk, wink
XT	next, text
SK	ask, bask, cask, desk, disk, dusk, husk, mask, musk, risk, task, tusk
SP	asp, cusp, gasp, lisp, rasp, wisp
ST	best, bust, cast, cost, dust, fast, fist, gust, jest, just, last, list, lost, mast, mist, must, nest, past, pest, rest, rust, test, vast, vest, west, zest

SH	ash, bash, cash, dish, fish, gash, gosh, gush, lash, lush, mash, mush, posh, rash, rush, sash, wish
TH	bath, math, moth, path, with

Notes:

The two above, SH and TH, are not actually two different sounds like the previous words. S and H together make one specific sound. T and H together make one specific sound. But your student will have to learn these blends at some point. Now is a good time.

Notice that I have omitted words like mold, cold or bank, because they have long vowels and we are still focusing on only short vowels.

*The corresponding First Step Phonics books for these consonant blends are **Level 2, Set 2**. Workbook is **Level 2, Workbook 2**.*

Notes:

After your student can seamlessly blend two consonants at the end of words, the next step is to conquer words with two consonant sounds at the beginning, such as: stop, brat, grub, prep, et cetera.

Here is a list of words with two consonants in the beginning. Note that this list also includes two consonants that make *one* sound (ch, sh, th).

BL	bled, blip, blob, blog, blot
BR	brad, brag, bran, brat, brig, brim
CL	clad, clap, clam, clan, clef, clip, clod, clog, clop, clot
CR	crab, cram, crib, crop, crud
DR	drab, drag, dreg, drib, drip, drop, drug, drum
FL	flag, flap, flat, fled, flex, flip, flog, flop, flub, flux
FR	fret, friz, frog
GL	glad, glam, glen, glob, glug, glum, glut
GR	grab, grad, gram, gran, grim, grin, grip, grit, grub
PL	plan, pled, plod, plop, plot, plug, plus, plum
PR	prep, prod, prop
QU	quid, quip, quit, quiz
SC	scab, scad, scag, scam, scan, scat, scud, scum
SK	skid, skim, skin, skip
SL	slab, slam, slap, slat, sled, slid, slim, slip, slit, slob, slop, slot, slug, slum
SM	smog, smug

SN	snag, snap, snip, snit, snob, snot, snub
SP	spam, span, spat, sped, spin, spit, spot, spud, spun
ST	stab, stag, step, stop, stub, stun
SW	swag, swam, swig
TR	tram, trap, trim, trip, trod, trot
TW	twig, twin, twit
CH	chap, chat, chin, chip, chop, chub, chug, chum
SH	shag, sham, shed, shin, ship, shop, shot, shun, shut
TH	than, that, them, then, thin, this, thud, thug, thus

Notes:

Note that QU is listed in this section with consonant blends because when U is used with Q, U usually makes the W sound. When making the W sound, U is a consonant and, therefore, QU is a consonant blend.

*The corresponding First Step Phonics books for these consonant blends are **Level 2, Set 3**. Workbook is **Level 2, Workbook 3**.*

Notes:

Gradually move up to five-letter words with two-letter consonant blends at both the beginning and end of the word, such as blond, stand, flint, clump, blend, et cetera.

Following is a list of words with two consonants together at both the beginning and at the end.

BL	black, blast, bless, blimp, blink, block, blond, bluff, blunt
BR	brand, brick, bring, brink, brisk, brunt
CL	clamp, clash, class, click, cliff, cling, clink, clock, clomp, clonk, cloth, cluck, clung, clunk
CR	crack, cramp, crash, crept, crimp, crisp, cross, crush, crust
DR	draft, dress, drift, drill, drink, drunk
FL	flash, flask, fleck, flesh, flick, fling, flint, flock, fluff, flump, flush
FR	fresh, frill, frisk, frizz, frock, frost, froth
GL	gland, glass, glint, glitz, gloss
GR	graft, grand, grant, grasp, grass, grift, grill, grunt
PL	plant, plink, plonk, plump, pluck, plush
PR	press, prick, primp, print
QU	quack, quell, quest, quick, quill, quilt
SC	scalp, scamp, scant, scuff
SK	skill, skimp, skull, skunk
SL	slack, slash, sling, slink, slosh, sloth, slump, slung, slush
SM	smack, smash, smell, smelt, smith, smock, smush

SN	snack, sniff, snuff
SP	speck, spell, spend, spent, spill, spunk
ST	staff, stamp, stand, stick, stiff, still, stilt, sting, stink, stock, stomp, stuck, stuff, stump, stunk, stunt
SW	swell, swept, swift, swill, swing, swish, swiss, swung
TR	track, tract, tramp, trash, trick, truck, trump, trunk, trust
TW	twill, twist
CH	champ, chant, check, chess, chest, chick, chill, chimp, chomp, chuck, chump, chunk
SH	shack, shaft, shock, shuck, shush
TH	theft, thing, think, thong, thump, thunk

Notes:

*The corresponding First Step Phonics books for these consonant blends are **Level 2, Set 4**. Workbook is **Level 2, Workbook 4**.*

Tip #1:

Don't include PH (*phone*) or GH (*laugh*) words that make the F sound since many of those words also contain other complications that shouldn't be included in this level. Also, there are very few of these types of words. These letter blends can be taught later when they are encountered.

Tip #2:

Remember that regardless of the level you're working on, you can engage your student in any of the activities or games explained in Part II of this manual.

The final step for consonant blends is words that have three consonants in a row, like bench, strict, squish, shrimp, thrust, et cetera.

Here is a list of words:

NCH	bench, blanch, branch, brunch, bunch, clinch, crunch, french, grinch, lunch, munch, stench, trench
SCR	scram, scrap, scrimp, script, scrub, scruff, scrunch
SHR	shred, shrill, shrimp, shrink, shrub, shrug, shrunk
SPL	splat, splash, split, splint, splotch
SQU	squid, squint, squish
SPR	sprig, spring, sprint, sprung
STR	strand, strap, strep, strict, string, strip, strong, struck, strum, strung, strut
THR	thrash, thresh, thrift, thrill, throb, throng, thrust
TCH	batch, blotch, clutch, crutch, etch, fetch, glitch, itch, hatch, hitch, hutch, latch, match, patch, pitch, scratch, sketch, snatch, snitch, splotch, stitch, stretch, switch, twitch, witch

Don't forget to test your student at the end of each level with made-up words. Some fake words for this level could be GRILCH, BRIMP, FLUNCH, et cetera. If they can pronounce those, it's a pass.

*The corresponding First Step Phonics books for these consonant blends are **Level 2, Set 5**. Workbook is **Level 2, Workbook 5**.*

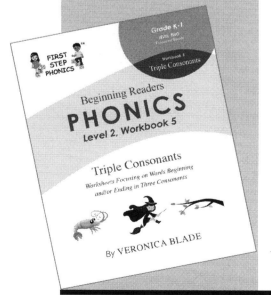

A long vowel is when the sound of the vowel is pronounced like the name of a letter. For instance, the vowel sound in STREET is long E which sounds like the name of E. This step is dedicated to words ending in E, which is an easy first step to learning long vowels. A simple way to explain this is: "The E at the end makes the first vowel say its name."

I usually start off by writing a word like CUB and getting them to read it. Then I add the E at the end. As I say the new word, I draw out the name of the U to make sure they hear the difference. Do this with a variety of words with an E at the end in which the vowel has the long sound.

Here is a list of the three-letter words, which turn into long vowels after adding an E at the end.

A

cap to cape	nap to nape
can to cane	pal to pale
fat to fate	pan to pane
mad to made	rat to rate
man to mane	sat to sate
mat to mate	

Notes:

Notes:

E

pet to Pete   met to mete

I

bid to bide   hid to hide

pin to pine   sit to site

rid to ride   Tim to time

dim to dime   tin to tine

din to dine   kit to kite

fin to fine   win to wine

rip to ripe

O

cod to code	mop to mope
con to cone	nod to node
cop to cope	not to note
dot to dote	rob to robe
hop to hope	rod to rode
lob to lobe	rot to rote
lop to lope	tot to tote
mod to mode	

Notes:

U

cub to cube	dud to dude
cut to cute	tub to tube

Notes:

This rule also applies to words with consonant blends, such as:

past to paste

shin to shine

slid to slide

bath to bathe

sham to shame

plan to plane

The above should give your student a pretty good idea without providing bigger words. But if you're student is more advanced, use your own judgement.

Before going on to the next step, give your student made-up test words to sound out, like PABE, MEVE, GROME, CLISHE, STROFE, STRAME, FLUDE, et cetera. If they can easily read those, continue to the next level.

*After they have the above concept, the corresponding First Step Phonics books for this step are **Level 3, Set 1**. Workbook is **Level 3, Workbook 1**.*

Step 12: Vowel blends

Vowel blends are a combination of vowels that make one sound, such as EE and EA, which both make the long E sound. You don't have to say "long E" though. You can use the phrase "the vowel is saying its name." Explain long vowels whichever way you think will be easier for your student to understand.

There are many more vowel blends, such as OO, which has four different sounds (boom, blood, door, cook), or OU which has three different sounds (our, four, you). And then there are the vowel-consonant blends that act as a single vowel sound, such as OW which can be pronounced two ways (cow, low) or AW (paw).

Y can also act as a vowel. Note that Y can make the long E sound, such as at the end of words like happy. However, they are usually multisyllable words, which is why this sound is not covered until a later step in this manual.

This step should also include vowel-R words, which make their own distinct sounds: AR, ER, IR, OR and UR.

I have included a list, but did not include multisyllable words or words with meanings that are too complex.

Please be sure not to throw all the following blends at your student at one time. Start with EE and let your student read some of those words. Have them do some spelling, use alphabet cards, and play games. Get your student to write out sentences you dictate and find books focusing on EE. Then repeat those activities with EA. Get in as much practice with each blend as you can before introducing a new vowel blend.

Notes:

Tip #1:

Note: When EA and AI are followed by an R (as in the last two rows on this page), the dictionary does not say it's pronounced as short E. But it will sound to your student enough like short E to get your student to pronounce the word correctly. At this stage, teaching it as short E will keep it simple. This also applies to words on page 48 (fourth row) being taught as long O (*your*, *court*).

Long E

EE	bee, see, fee, tee, gee, wee, beef, beep, beet, deed, deep, feed, feel, flee, free, geek, glee, heed, heel, jeep, keel, keen, keep, leek, meek, meet, need, peek, peel, peep, reed, reef, reek, reel, seed, seek, seem, seen, seep, teem, teen, tree, weed, week, weep, cheek, bleed, breed, bleep, creek, creep, freeze, fleet, geese, greed, queen, sheep, sheen, sheet, sleep, sleet, speed, spree, steel, steep, sweep, sweet, teeth, three, tweed, tweet, screen, spleen, street
EA	sea, eat, tea, pea, bead, beak, beam, bean, beat, deal, dean, each, ease, east, eave, feat, flea, heal, heap, heat, jean, lead, leaf, leak, lean, leap, mean, meal, meat, neat, peak, plea, read, real, ream, seal, seam, seat, teak, teal, team, teat, veal, weak, wean, zeal, beach, bleak, bleat, cease, cheap, clean, cheat, cleat, creak, cream, dream, freak, gleam, glean, leach, lease, leash, least, leave, peach, sneak, speak, steal, steam, teach, tease, tweak, weave
IE	brief, chief, field, fiend, grief, lien, shield, thief, wield, yield

Short E

EA	dead, deaf, head, bear, pear, tear, wear, dealt, meant, realm, swear, sweat
AI	said, pair, hair, air, flair, fair, lair, stair, chair

Long A

AI	aid, aim, bail, fail, gain, gait, hail, jail, laid, lain, maid, mail, maim, main, nail, paid, pail, pain, raid, rail, rain, sail, tail, wail, wait, braid, brain, chain, claim, drain, faint, faith, flail, frail, grain, paint, plain, quail, saint, snail, stain, taint, train, trait, waist, waive
AY	aye, bay, day, gay, hay, may, pay, ray, say, way, clay, fray, gray, play, pray, quay, slay, spay, stay, sway, tray, spray, stray

Long I

IE	die, fie, lie, pie, tie, vie, cried, cries, dried, flies, fries, pried, plied, shied, spies, tried
Y	cry, dry, fly, fry, ply, pry, shy, sky, sly, spy, sty, thy, try, why, wry, spry

Short O

AU	aunt, daub, haul, maul, cause, daunt, fraud, gaunt, gauze, haunt, jaunt, mauve, pause, vault, taunt
AW	aw, awe, caw, haw, jaw, law, maw, paw, raw, saw, bawl, claw, craw, dawn, draw, fawn, flaw, gawk, hawk, lawn, pawn, slaw, yawn, brawl, brawn, crawl, drawl, drawn, shawl, spawn, squaw, straw

Notes:

47

Notes:

Long O

OA	oat, boat, coal, coat, coax, foal, foam, goal, goat, hoax, load, loaf, loan, moan, oath, road, roam, roan, soak, soap, toad, bloat, boast, cloak, coach, coast, croak, float, poach, roast
OE	doe, foe, hoe, Joe, roe, toe, goes, sloe
OW	low, mow, own, row, tow, blow, bowl, crow, glow, grow, mown, show, slow, snow, sown, stow, blown, flown, grown, shown, throw
OU	four, your, soul, court, mourn

Miscellaneous O Sounds

OI	boil, coif, coil, coin, foil, join, oink, roil, soil, toil, void, broil, droid, foist, groin, hoist, joint, joist, moist, poise, spoil
OY	boy, coy, joy, soy, toy, ploy, Troy
OO	blood, flood
OO	book, cook, foot, good, hood, hoof, hook, look, nook, took, woof, wood, wool, brook, crook, shook, stood
OU	our, out, bout, foul, gout, hour, loud, lout, noun, ouch, pout, rout, sour, thou, tout, bound, cloud, couch, count, flour, found, ground, hound, house, mouse, mouth, pound, pouch, round, roust, scour, scout, shout, snout, south, spout, trout, vouch
OW	cow, how, now, owl, pow, sow, vow, wow, brow, chow, down, fowl, gown, howl, jowl, plow, town, yowl, brown, clown, crowd, crown, drown, frown

OO	boo, coo, goo, moo, ooh, too, poo, woo, zoo, boob, boom, boot, cool, coop, coot, doom, food, fool, goof, goon, goop, loom, loop, loot, mood, moon, moot, noon, poof, pool, pooh, poop, room, soon, tool, toot, zoom, bloom, drool, droop, gloom, goose, groom, proof, scoop, shoot, spoof, spook, spool, spoon, stool, stoop, swoon, swoop, tooth, troop, vroom
UE	cue, due, hue, rue, sue, blue, clue, flue, glue, true
EW	dew, ewe, few, hew, mew, new, pew, yew, blew, brew, chew, crew, flew, grew, stew, threw
OU	you, youth, wound, croup, group

Vowel-R Blends

AR	arc, ark, art, bar, car, far, jar, mar, par, tar, arch, barb, bard, barf, bark, barn, card, carp, cart, char, dark, darn, dart, farm, fart, garb, hard, hark, harm, harp, hart, lard, lark, mark, mart, park, part, scar, spar, star, tarp, tart, arm, yard, yarn, chard, charm, chart, march, marsh, parch, shard, shark, sharp, smart, stark, start
OR	or, for, nor, orb, born, cord, cork, corn, dork, dorm, ford, fork, form, fort, horn, lord, morn, norm, port, sort, torn, tort, worn
OR	word, worm, work, world
ER	her, per, fern, germ, herb, herd, jerk, nerd, perk, perm, pert, term, verb, clerk, nerve, serve, terse, twerp, verse

Continued on the next page.

Notes:

49

Notes:

IR	fir, irk, sir, bird, dirt, firm, girl, stir, birch, birth, chirp, girth, quirk, shirt, skirt, smirk, swirl, third, twirl, whirl
UR	cur, fur, urn, blur, burn, burp, burr, curb, curd, curl, curt, furl, hurl, hurt, lurk, purr, slur, spur, surf, turf, turn, blurb, blurt, burst, churn, curse, curve, lurch, nurse, purse, slurp, spurn, church

Occasionally, you'll find one or two words that don't fit any rules, like *friend* which may be the only IE word with the short E sound. We are at the mercy of the English language.

Look for reading books with simple words where each book concentrates on only one or two blends. Also, as with the previous steps, have them read made-up words to ensure they have had enough practice with the above vowel blends.

*You can find the corresponding First Step Phonics books and workbooks for vowel blends in **Level 4**.*

Step 13: Multiple syllables

The next several steps in this manual involve multiple-syllable words. A syllable is a series of letters that make its own set of sounds which contain only one vowel sound. When you move to another part of the word with a new and separate vowel sound, you have to rearrange a part of your mouth to make that new sound. Each time you rearrange for that new sound, you are saying a new syllable.

Give your student some examples and make sure your student also gives plenty of examples.

I have collected some fairly simple words (next page) that do not have sound elements beyond what we have covered in this book. Have your student write the number of syllables in each blank space.

Notes:

How many syllables are in each word?

_____ murder

_____ darken

_____ after

_____ under

_____ kitten

_____ timid

_____ account

_____ inquire

_____ difficult

_____ investigate

_____ winter

_____ snippet

_____ current

_____ outcast

_____ monster

_____ frequent

_____ strict

_____ tomorrow

_____ important

_____ remote

_____ quilt

_____ sailboat

_____ volcano

_____ octopus

_____ hexagon

_____ window

_____ kitchen

_____ clock

_____ masterful

_____ spectacular

How many syllables are in each word?

_____ shampoo	_____ gossip
_____ shorts	_____ athlete
_____ basket	_____ director
_____ morning	_____ collect
_____ frolic	_____ coffee
_____ underground	_____ agenda
_____ rainbow	_____ maintain
_____ supper	_____ bookshelf
_____ calendar	_____ apartment
_____ computer	_____ scalp
_____ scarlet	_____ dictionary
_____ greenhouse	_____ communicate
_____ street	_____ television
_____ peacock	_____ excuse
_____ dragonfly	_____ stripe

Notes:

At this stage, your student should be able to read the majority of words in children's books. Have your student select multisyllable words from those books and then tell you how many syllables are in each word. Have your student name objects around the house and tell you the number of syllables in each word. You can probably find free downloadable worksheets by doing an internet search.

I have no corresponding workbooks for this step, or the next several steps in this manual, since plenty of material already exists elsewhere that covers the more difficult words.

Reminder: Make sure you have your student do plenty of spelling with the words from this and all the next steps. You can use single words or have them write entire sentences that you dictate. This will help create more awareness of the words.

Step 14: The Schwa

With multiple syllables often comes the schwa. A simple way of explaining this: schwa is an unaccented syllable where the vowel has no distinct sound (except to maybe sound a little like short U). Another way of explaining it is that the schwa is a syllable that you're not saying as much, or not stressing as hard, as other parts of the word.

In the word animal, the last syllable is the schwa. In the word normal, again the last syllable. The schwa is in the first syllable of the word again. Other examples: difficult, absolute, giggle, amid, Amelia, telephone.

Have your student find the schwa in each word on the next page.

Tip #1
If you're not sure of the schwa in any of the words, you can verify it by looking in a dictionary.

Where is the schwa in each word?

_____	murder	_____	after
_____	account	_____	difficult
_____	current	_____	monster
_____	frequent	_____	tomorrow
_____	hexagon	_____	adept
_____	bottom	_____	masterful
_____	lemon	_____	person
_____	survive	_____	wizard
_____	rainbow	_____	supper
_____	computer	_____	system
_____	harmony	_____	postman
_____	gossip	_____	alone
_____	present	_____	reason
_____	garden	_____	custom
_____	student	_____	instant

Where is the schwa in each word?

_____	balance	_____	human
_____	winter	_____	zebra
_____	kitchen	_____	fragile
_____	octopus	_____	carnival
_____	habit	_____	criminal
_____	woman	_____	estimate
_____	focus	_____	helicopter
_____	underground	_____	original
_____	calendar	_____	unity
_____	medium	_____	chemical
_____	dragonfly	_____	musical
_____	director	_____	cavity
_____	America	_____	medical
_____	problem	_____	similar
_____	division	_____	president

Step 15: When Y, C, and G sounds change

Notes:

The C sound usually changes to the soft sound when followed by an E, I, or Y.

CE	cede, cell, cent, cease, cedar, center, cellar, censor, census
CI	cite, cider, cigar, cilia, cinch, civic, civil, citrus
CY	cyan, cyst, cycle, cyber, cyborg, cyclic, cymbal

The sound of G often, but not always, changes to the soft G sound when followed by an E.

GE	gee, gel, gem, gent, gene, age, cage, gage, huge, page, rage, sage, urge, wage, binge, bulge, stage, surge, verge

The sound of Y often becomes long E when at the end of words.

Y	any, icy, ivy, army, body, bony, boxy, cozy, duly, duty, easy, envy, gory, hazy, holy, icky, jury, lacy, lady, lazy, lily, navy, nosy, oily, only, pity, puny, rosy, ruby, tidy, tiny, ugly, very, happy.

Step 16: Other sound blends

The next step would be teaching your student about words with multiple-letter combinations that have specific sounds, such as words ending in ION (onion), OUS (glorious) and how the CI, SI or TI (gracious, session, friction) makes the SH sound.

The words for these higher levels can be difficult and tend to have more complex meanings. Only you can decide which ones your student can handle. Skip any words with meanings you feel will be too hard to explain.

Notes:

ION (sounds like YUN)	onion, union, opinion, reunion, dominion, communion, companion
TION (sounds like SHUN)	action, lotion, motion, nation, option, potion, ration, auction, caption, caution, diction, edition, elation, emotion, faction, fiction, mention, ovation, portion, section, station, suction, tuition
SION (sounds like SHUN)	fusion, lesion, vision, erosion, evasion, fission, mansion, mission, passion, pension, session, tension, version, abrasion, adhesion, aversion, cohesion, decision, delusion, division, emission, illusion, incision, invasion, occasion, omission, revision

Continued on the next page.

Notes:

OUS (sounds like US)	famous, joyous, odious, porous, amorous, curious, devious, envious, furious, hideous, jealous, nervous, obvious, ominous, serious, tedious, various, zealous
CIOUS (sounds like SHUS)	vicious, gracious, luscious, precious, spacious, conscious, delicious, ferocious, judicious, malicious, vivacious, suspicious
TIOUS (sounds like SHUS)	cautious, seditious, ambitious, fictitious, infectious, nutritious
TURE (sounds like CHER)	future, nature, capture, culture, denture, feature, fixture, gesture, lecture, mixture, nurture, pasture, picture, posture, rapture, rupture, stature, texture, torture, venture, vulture, creature, fracture, mature, juncture, moisture, puncture, tincture
LE (sounds like just L)	able, axle, idle, amble, ample, angle, ankle, apple, bible, bugle, cable, cycle, eagle, fable, gable, ladle, maple, noble, rifle, sable, table, title, uncle, battle, beagle, beetle, bridle, candle, cattle, cuddle, dimple, double, couple

Step 17: Words ending in ED

Your student needs to learn the sounds of ED (past tense) at the end of words, and when they are pronounced differently. The three pronunciations are D, T, and ID.

If the word ends with a T or D sound, you pronounce ED as ID. For example, padded is pronounced PADDID. Here are more examples:

D	faded, pleaded, beaded, landed, folded, needed, wanted, hooded, graded, loaded, crowded, guided
T	listed, patted, mated, halted, waited, wanted, fretted, texted, hated, muted, cited

If you don't use your voice at the end of the word, the ED doesn't have a voice either. For example, in the word tuck, you are not using your voice for the K sound so the ED is pronounced as the sound of T. Tucked would be pronounced TUKT. Here are more examples:

P	helped, clapped, shopped, zipped, moped, draped, dripped
F	laughed, coughed, toughed, roughed, miffed, cuffed, knifed
S	hissed, kissed, passed, bossed, fussed, tossed, iced, sliced
SH	fished, dashed, gushed, hushed, wished, bashed

Continued on the next page.

Notes:

Notes:

CH	latched, hitched, fetched, sketched, twitched, matched, botched
K	ducked, blocked, licked, hacked, parked, picked, puked, liked
X	maxed, fixed, mixed, vexed, faxed, waxed, nixed, coaxed

If you're using your voice at the end of the word, then you would use your voice for ED too. For example, you are using your voice for the N in tan, so the ED at the end is pronounced as the sound of D. Tanned is pronounced TAND. Here are more examples:

B	bobbed, troubled, nabbed, stabbed, cubed, probed, clubbed
G	gagged, logged, clogged, hogged, lagged, mugged, hugged
L	willed, pulled, killed, fooled, called, paled, hauled, filed, nailed
M	bombed, formed, calmed, aimed, crammed, hemmed
N	canned, opened, lined, planned, gained, burned, honed, joined
R	floored, scared, mired, cured, mattered, scored, erred, mirrored
V	revved, caved, lived, strived, loved, moved, gloved, shaved
W	vowed, followed, bellowed, viewed, mowed, flawed, pawed

| Y | played, strayed, splayed, deployed, annoyed, grayed, toyed |
| Z | fizzed, buzzed, whizzed, frizzed, quizzed, razzed, jazzed |

Since you will need to explain that ED tells us something has happened in the past, you can go over ING words as well. Cover the pronunciation, but also explain that ING at the end of words shows something happening in the present time.

Notes:

Step 18: Silent letters

Notes:

Next, go over these silent letters with your student; otherwise, they will try to pronounce these letters in future words.

GH	sigh, fight, light, right, night, tight, bright, flight, fright, aught, caught, though, thought, through, drought, straight, neighbor, twilight, daughter, slaughter, naughty, doughnut
K	knob, knot, knee, kneel, knit, know, knife, knock, knoll, knight, knuckle, knowledge
B	comb, bomb, crumb, limb, lamb, thumb, numb, climb, womb, jamb, debt, doubt, subtle, plumber
H	heir, hour, honest, honor, ghost, ghastly, aghast, ghetto, ghoul, rhyme, ache, echo, chaos, choir, chord, scheme, chrome, school, stomach, monarchy, character, charisma, chemical, chlorine, what, where, when, while, white, why
W	who, whom, wrap, wring, wreck, wrist, wreath, wrench, wretch, wrong, write, wrinkle, wrestle, two, answer, sword
G	gnu, gnaw, gnome, gnash, gnat
L	palm, calm, walk, talk, chalk, stalk, calf, half, should, could
T	often, soften, listen, fasten, ballet, fillet, castle, hustle, whistle, wrestle, nestle, glisten, moisten
N	damn, autumn, column, condemn, hymn, solemn

You may come across more of these oddities. Such is the English language that is a combination of so many other languages and rules.

Step 19: Double consonants and short vowels

On multiple-syllable words, how does one know whether to pronounce the vowel as long or short? The general rule is that when you have one consonant, the vowel will usually be long. When you see a double consonant, the vowel sound will usually be short.

Here are some examples:

cable vs. babble

bible vs. bubble

ladle vs. saddle

idle vs. paddle

rifle vs. ruffle

trifle vs. truffle

ogle vs. giggle

tiger vs. trigger

silo vs. silly

pilot vs. ballot

tamer vs. hammer

Notes:

pony vs. skinny

zany vs. funny

caper vs. capper

sniper vs. slipper

nasal vs. lasso

bison vs. lesson

title vs. cattle

later vs. latter

crazy vs. dazzle

I have included as many consonant and vowel combinations as possible. But, as with all rules in the English language, these rules may vary.

Step 20: Basic Punctuation

Since this manual is not intended as a grammar lesson, we are only covering the most commonly used punctuation that a newer reader might encounter. Although I have placed this section at the end, you can teach it any time after Step 12. Be sure to have your student make plenty of examples. You can write sentences and the student must place the punctuation in the correct position or the student can spot examples in books or you can find worksheets online.

PERIOD

"A mark (.) used to signal the end of a sentence."

Examples: The dog is furry. Cake is delicious.

COMMA

"A mark (,) used to show a pause in a sentence or to separate parts of a sentence."

Examples: I like shorts, not pants. He loves peas, corn, and string beans.

QUESTION MARK

"A mark (?) used to show a question is being asked."

Examples: How was your day? May I have more ice cream?

Notes:

Notes:

EXCLAMATION POINT

"A mark (!) used to show emotion."

Examples: Hey, that's great! I love it!

APOSTROPHE

"A mark (') used to show missing letters or that something belongs to something else."

Examples of missing letters: can't, wouldn't, hadn't

Examples of belonging: My mother's cooking made me happy. The dog's ear is hairy.

QUOTATION MARKS

"Marks ("") used to show the exact words said."

Examples: "Where are you going?" he asked. "Please sit," she told me.

We have reached the end of the phonics steps. I hope this manual has helped you. May your new reader learn quickly and enjoy every minute of it!

See the next section for rules to the games and activities mentioned earlier in this book.

Part II Activities

Part II: Activities

Spelling

This is self-explanatory. You say the sound or word, and the student writes it. You can work out a point system with a reward at the end. For instance, every time they spell something correctly, they get a point. You can set a goal, and when they meet that goal, they get to play one of the other games below.

I strongly recommend you work on spelling during every single step of this phonics program, even if your student is writing only one letter. This develops the ability to hear sounds and then translate those sounds into words and sentences. It also improves the student's spelling and writing skills.

Forming or Building

Make the letter in clay, Play-Doh, draw it in sand or dirt, color it, fold a paper into the shape, create the shape using building blocks, et cetera. If you don't have clay or Play-Doh, you can find recipes online for moldable substances. Forming the letter helps cement the letter or word in their mind.

Ask your student occasionally what letter or word they are making.

Alphabet cards

You can purchase alphabet cards or create them using heavy cardstock and a marker. I highly recommend alphabet cards, because they can be quite useful, inexpensive and fun. With a little imagination, alphabet cards can go a long way. Here are some suggestions:

- Decide in advance how many points must be reached to end the game. You flash the card and the student tells you what it is. If the student's answer is correct, he gets a point. Depending on how proficient he is on the current step, you could take away one point when he answers incorrectly.

- Mix up the alphabet cards and have the student put them in alphabetical order.

- Remove some of the letters while keeping the rest in sequence, then mix up the removed letters and have the student put them where they belong.

- If you have two sets, you can play Go Fish or Concentraion and collect pairs of the letters.

- If you have an uppercase deck and a lowercase deck, your student can match uppercase to lowercase during Go Fish or Concentration.

Whatever game you are playing or whatever level your student is learning, you can occasionally get tricky and choose an incorrect card to help build your student's awareness. If he catches it, he gets a point.

Slap

This game works only on the very young, and you'll see why in a moment. Decide in advance how many points the winner must reach to win. Keep in mind that the younger the child, the shorter the attention span. I suggest starting with five or so points for very young students.

Four alphabet cards are laid faceup so both of you can see the letters. You call out the letter or sound and whoever slaps it first

Notes:

gets the point. You know which one you're going to call out, and so you have the advantage. Luckily, this never occurs to the younger ones. When they win, they believe they truly won. Let them believe it. I promise it won't hurt them in any way. :)

Make sure to let the student win most of the Slap games, because when they are very young, they can get deflated in a blink of an eye. But you should win a game here and there too.

Slap can be played with letters to practice the names or to practice the sounds. You can also make alphabet cards with vowel-consonant or consonant-vowel blends, and eventually move up to three-letter words.

Concentration

The goal of Concentration is to acquire pairs, so you will need two sets of whatever you are working on. With letters, I suggest using one set of uppercase and another set of lowercase. The student can match them. But only do that if your student has already learned both.

Since there are twenty-six letters in the alphabet and you need two of each, I suggest limiting the cards to just eight or nine letters for a total of sixteen or eighteen cards. If the child is very young, you might want to limit it to five letters which would make ten cards.

Cards are placed facedown so neither of you can see the letter. When I played with a child, it wasn't about me, so I always let the student go first. The student turns over two cards. If the cards match, the student gets to keep the two cards and take another turn. When two cards are turned over that don't match, they flip the cards facedown again and their turn is over. Coach your student to remember where those letters are.

The next person turns over two cards. If they match, he gets to keep them. If they don't match, he flips them facedown and his turn is over. When all the cards are gone, whoever has the most pairs is the winner. Don't worry about this game not being productive enough. It is! It develops memory, letter recognition, and problem solving.

When you are playing with children, I urge you to forget which letters are where. If your student loses too often, he won't want to play again and you lose a great way to help him learn.

Go Fish

There are various versions of this game, but we are only concerned with the simplest. And even then, we are simplifying it more. Real versions call for collecting sets of four of a kind, but we are only collecting pairs.

As with Concentration, you'll need pairs of alphabet cards. And to prevent the child from being overwhelmed, start with two sets of half the alphabet, which would be twenty-six alphabet cards. Or, if your student is very young, use only about a third of the alphabet (sixteen to eighteen cards) or fewer. Pass out five or so cards to each player, then set the rest between you and the student. Let the student go first.

The students must have in their hand anything they request of you. They would ask, "Do you have a T?" and if you have it, you hand it over. They add that pair to their winnings and get to go again. If the student asks for something which you do not have, you tell them, "Go fish," and they pick up a card from the top of the deck. If the student gets the card just asked of you, they put the pair aside, and their turn continues. When they don't get what was requested, they draw, and then it's your turn. When the deck runs out, whoever has the most pairs wins the game.

Notes:

Role Reversal

Role reversal is exactly what it sounds like, and it doesn't cost you a dime. Let your student be the teacher and you the student. You can do this with Concentration, Go Fish, spelling, or alphabet cards. You spell a word, or hand over a Go Fish card, et cetera, and let him figure out if you did it correctly. When the student makes a correct call, they get a point. When they make a bad call, you get a point. Before you start, set a point goal.

Another activity similar to role reversal is to lay out the alphabet cards face up. Point to a card (like the letter B, for instance) and ask him or her questions like, "Is this a B?" You can also say an incorrect letter. If your student gives the correct answer, he or she gets a point.

I have found role reversal to be invaluable. By being the teacher, the student must watch carefully and give more consideration to your answers. It gives them more awareness of the subject and helps them develop critical thinking.

Bingo

Print and cut all 26 letters and place the 26 pieces of paper in a bowl. Give each player a bingo card. The teacher randomly draws one of the pieces of paper and calls out the letter to the players. Players mark off the coordinating square for that letter. A player wins when five squares in a row are marked off, either vertical, horizontal or diagonal. Download and print bingo cards for free at FirstStepPhonics.com.

Part III Tips for Success

Part III: Tips for Success

Notes:

A Well-Rested and Well-Fed Student

Ensuring the student has eaten well is just as important as anything else you do in any study endeavor. Not only will hunger distract him, but nutritious food gives him the physical and mental energy to learn. Avoid foods or drinks with processed sugar as they have been proven to interfere with one's concentration and/or can cause your student to become agitated or restless. After the sugar high wears off, students often become sluggish.

Make sure your student has had enough sleep. If your student is tired, something that may normally be easy to grasp could quickly become frustrating for both of you. At the very least, being tired will slow your student down.

Always make sure the student is fresh and ready to learn before you start any lesson.

Interest, Purpose, and Goals

Your student being engaged is vital to learning. The student should be curious, even if only a little, about whatever course of study they are about to embark. If they see no purpose for learning a subject, you will probably get less of their attention. They will quickly become bored, fidgety, or uncooperative. That will make the process more difficult for everyone.

Perhaps your child wants to be an actor when he or she grows up. In that case, actors must be able to read scripts. Maybe your student is obsessed with being a race car driver. First, one must get a driver's license and for that, one has to pass a written test. Anyone who wants to be a veterinarian will need reading skills to study about animals. A singer must be capable of reading music and lyrics. Your student may be competitive, and his inspiration may be to appear smarter than other kids. Or it may be as simple as a desire to read the words on a cereal box or video game.

Everyone has a purpose. Poke around until you find it. Engage your student's sense of curiosity. Instill a purpose. Set a goal.

Notes:

Praise vs. Criticism

Do you remember what it was like in the classroom with a stern teacher who scowled even though you answered her question or who could never be satisfied no matter how hard you worked? Did you have a teacher who got angry or impatient when you couldn't understand a concept?

Negativity can kill a child's passion or stifle their enthusiasm and only makes the experience less productive and less rewarding for everyone. If a student feels stressed, they won't progress as quickly.

Do you remember a time when someone encouraged you to learn, maybe told you how wonderfully you did something? After that, you could practically fly! When a person focuses on positive progress, better results are likelier to occur. Praise for a job well done can make one want to do even better. Just a few nice words can make a seemingly dull student brighten. Kindness is magical.

Also, remember to keep the many hats you wear separate. When you are teaching, you are not "Mom" or "Dad." Be the teacher. Even better, be the teacher who makes your student feel good about his or her accomplishments, no matter how small. Be the teacher you wish you had.

Setting the Duration of Lessons

You can generally expect your student's attention span to increase with age. The reverse is also true. Maybe your child is particularly motivated at four years old and can focus for a full fifteen minutes. But more likely, you'll have only five or ten minutes of intense learning before you have to switch to a lighter activity.

I usually worked with very young children in one-hour blocks, and the parents expected me to use that entire hour for learning—not an easy task. So I broke up the lessons, practicing sounds, then playing a game. Then I'd return to more serious phonics.

One thing is certain: if you turn learning into a stressful event, you won't get the results you hoped for. This philosophy is especially applicable to very young children. But even older students want studying to be pleasant. Switch things up often, moving from one activity to another. Keep it light. Keep it fun.

Notes:

Notes:

Schedule and Structure

I have found that children will almost always choose to play rather than do schoolwork. If you had a choice to play or work, what would you do?

I never left it up to the student. If I wanted their attention, I made deals with them. For instance, the bargain would involve intense learning for ten minutes, followed by ten minutes of phonics-related games. After an hour, they could take a break and do something completely different as a reward for their hard work.

If you have difficulty getting your student to put in the effort you would like, initiate a reward system where they participate for an agreed-upon amount of time, or work until they meet a goal, and then they get a reward at the end.

Memorizing vs. Understanding

Being capable of repeating a series of sounds, or memorizing a string of words is useful for some things, but does not guarantee any understanding of a subject.

A good example of this would be working with fractions. A child can robotically add 1/2 to 1/2, according to the method taught, and get one whole. But if he understands that 1/2 is one of two equal parts, he can more easily grasp the concept that .5 is the same amount as 1/2.

Another example would be memorizing facts to pass a test. If the person doesn't understand what they are memorizing, they will not be able to apply whatever they supposedly "learned."

Similarly, a child can memorize a series of letters and say the word. But that doesn't mean he understands how to read—as he will discover once he encounters an unfamiliar word and is unable to sound it out.

But if your student *understands* the sounds for each of those letters or the letter combinations, they can sound out the majority of new words on their own.

Notes:

Examples and Practice

Use examples from real life and from your student's imagination. Or yours. It all works! The more your student practices or uses something, the more solid the student's understanding will be. And the higher the possibility your student will retain what he or she learned.

Let's say, for instance, your student has a pet golden retriever. If you ask them to describe the breed, they will easily describe the dog to you in detail, even years later. But if you tell them about a more obscure breed and ask them about it a week later, they probably won't remember much. More practice or exposure to anything will give you a better understanding and the more it is cemented in their minds.

If you find that your student seems to be losing progress or slowing down, back up and check the most recent steps. Very likely, you will discover that they missed getting the full understanding of something earlier. They probably need more examples or a little more practice with one of those steps. Once you fix that, the later steps will go smoother. The more your student comprehends the previous section, the easier it is to understand the next section.

Don't be in a hurry to push your student to the next step. Everyone learns at a different speed. Learning isn't a contest. It takes as long as it takes. Be prepared to stay on one step long after you're ready to move on.

Specialized Words for Reading

Every subject has its own set of words with special meanings that pertain to that subject. For example, a mechanic must be able to name the parts of an engine as well as understand how each thing works. A doctor must know the names to parts of the body and their functions in order to diagnose or cure. Similarly, the beginner reader needs to know the meaning of "word" and "letter," et cetera, if they want to truly understand what they are learning to do.

You wouldn't want to teach these words to a young reader straight from the dictionary since this can lead to other confusions. In this section, I provide simple ways to explain the words.

But before we cover that, you should make sure *you* understand what the word *teach* means. *Teach* means to instruct or share knowledge. When you teach your student, you are showing them how to do something and sharing what you know. *Teach* comes from Old English meaning to show.

Most importantly, you should understand what *phonetics* means since that's what you are teaching. *Phonetics* is the system of sounds for a language. For English, it's letters A through Z and the sounds that go with them. The system of sounds for English also includes consonant blends (for instance CH, SH, or TH, et cetera), vowel blends (such as OU, OE, EA, et cetera), letter combinations like TION or the various rules for the sounds of ED in past tense words. *Phonetic* comes from Greek meaning voice or sound.

Lastly, if you're going to teach your student about consonants, you need to be able to explain how some consonants require voice and some do not. When you use your voice, your vocal cords are active. When you're not using your voice, you are

Notes:

whispering. All vowels require use of your voice, but this is not a requirement with consonants. For instance, the sound for H requires no voice. Same with C, F, K, P, Q, S, T and X.

Many consonant sounds are similar to another letter, except one requires the use of your voice and the other does not. Examples of these similar consonants are F and V, K and G, P and B, S and Z, or T and D. You will read more on the differences between vowels and consonants in the next several pages.

Below is how I used to explain each meaning to the most common words for phonics. You can change or expand any of these, as needed, but try to work within the reality of your student's world. Also, it wouldn't hurt to review all these words in the beginning of each lesson. Do this until they no longer hesitate before telling you the meanings.

LETTER

"A shape that means a certain sound."

If your student already knows any letter sounds, use them as an example. If not, pick a simple consonant and give them tons of examples. D as in door, dog, dad, desk, dust, dark, duck, dish, dinner.

Try to choose things in your immediate environment that you can physically show them. You don't have to say the name of the letter at this stage if you don't want to. You can just draw it and then give examples of words that begin with that letter.

ALPHABET

"All the letters used in a language."

English has twenty-six letters, and they are the only letters used in our language. You can discuss other languages and how they have their own alphabet. Some languages have more letters, and they may look completely different from ours. Again, give your student examples. Do an internet search and actually look at other alphabets.

VOWEL

"A letter sound that is made without touching the tongue to any area of the mouth or moving the lips."

You would also add that with vowels, you are using your voice (as opposed to H where you are whispering). In other words, when you are making the vowel sound, your voice moves through your mouth without being stopped in any way.

The vowels are A, E, I, O, and U. But sometimes Y is a vowel, as in the word happy. Sometimes W is a vowel, as in the word saw. But I recommend covering only A, E, I, O, and U on this step, unless your student is more sophisticated.

You don't necessarily have to name the letters or show him the words. You could just make the sound as you

Tip #1:

I haven't always had success in explaining why H is a consonant and not a vowel. An internet search will give you multiple explanations on this and any of those could take you down a rabbit hole from which you may never escape. Rather than diving into any of that, you are probably better off avoiding it.

But if you can't go another minute without knowing for yourself, you can go to the Freebies page of FirstStepPhonics.com for a thorough explanation of H and why it is a consonant.

point to the actual thing. For example, if you are working on the letter A, drag out the short A sound as you point to the actual apple.

Don't forget to have him mimic the sounds you make.

CONSONANT

"A letter sound made by moving your lips or touching your tongue to the roof of your mouth or teeth, which changes the air flow through your mouth."

Start with the letter sounds where the student can watch the movement of your mouth, like the sounds for B, F, M, and P, then move on to the other letter sounds. Get them to make the sounds too, so they can see and feel for themselves.

WORD

"A group of letters or sounds that have a meaning. A word can be spoken or written."

I always found it easier to use examples nearby that the student could physically see. I would say the word while pointing at the thing that matched the word. Wall, floor, ceiling, door, table, book, paper, pencil. Say all those words and point to the item so your student understands that the words you say have a specific meaning. Get him to point to objects around the room and tell you the word that represents that object.

SENTENCE

"Words arranged that mean something and make sense or that have a complete thought."

Give him very simple examples, such as "The dog is white." Get him to see that you said a series of words that told a complete idea. Give him more examples. Get him to give you examples.

PERIOD

"A small dot at the end of a sentence that tells you it's the end of that thought or idea."

For very young students, I don't usually write sentences to use as examples. I say the sentence and tell them where the period would be. I would ask the students for examples too. However, if your student is more advanced, you can write the sentences with periods or have your student identify them in a book.

Notes:

READ

"To look at something and understand what it means."

This isn't necessarily limited to letters and words. You can read someone's lips or their expression. You can also read a posted sign that consists of only a picture.

You can draw a stop sign and get your student to tell you what it means. Put your index finger vertically across your lips and have them tell you what that means. Frown for your student and have them read your expression. If they can look at any of these things and understand the meaning, they're reading.

All that said, in some cases you aren't looking at something to get the meaning, like in braille when you are using your fingers. But most beginner readers don't need to know about braille.

Make sure the student gives you plenty of examples.

One thing people often miss is the purpose of reading which is to understand what you're seeing. If you don't understand the words, what is the point? School teaches you to guess the meaning of a word by the context. Guessing leaves room for error which could lead to misunderstanding the true meaning of sentences. Guessing is not knowing.

The real meaning of every single word encountered in any course of study is important and should be learned. Part of the learning process should be practicing the word in sentences until they can do it with ease. If the word can't be explained or used in a sentence, the word is probably not understood well enough. The student may need to be reminded of the meanings of some words more than once, and that's okay. Expanding your student's vocabulary and increasing their command of the language won't hurt them. I promise.

If any sample words provided earlier in this manual seem too complicated to explain, then skip them. There are plenty of others to choose from.

Notes:

Notes:

Let Your Student Work It Out

As tempting as it may be to blurt out answers to your student to speed things up, curb that urge when possible. Why would your student try to figure out the answer if he or she knows you will eventually provide it? People don't usually do anything if they don't have to.

If your student is truly stuck, ask questions or provide hints to get them thinking. Hold back on giving the answer unless you really need to. If you find you're providing answers too often, your student might have missed something. Try backing up and working on the previous step. When you return to the next step, you may find that your student has an easier time.

Activities and Games

Whether you're working with a younger child, a teenager, or an adult, always include other activities with the lesson (see Part II of this manual for ideas and tips). This is to keep the balance between words/concepts and the environment—connecting the subject to the real thing. Also, you may find, as I have, that changing activities keeps your student more alert.

If your student seems fuzzy or tired, have him draw pictures of the words. This gets the words out of his head and onto the paper. And if he is unable to draw it, he probably doesn't know what it means. That's your cue to explain it.

Other good activities are spelling and role reversal. Part II of this manual details these, as well as the rules for the games Slap, Concentration, and Go Fish.

Use real-life examples and things in the environment when possible. Learning is usually faster when the student can connect the subject to real life.

Notes:

Part IV Sample Lesson Plans

NOTE: The sample Lesson Plan is what a Lesson Plan *might* look like for a student who has learned uppercase letters but is still working on lowercase letters in Step 3. Since every student has their own individual needs, this sample should not be taken as a customized lesson for anyone. This is a sample only.

The first activity in every lesson should always include a review of the previous lesson. Any areas where the student seems slow or uncertain should be addressed immediately before advancing to later steps.

The blank Lesson Plan provided is intended to give you a way to list the activities the student needs to do during the next lesson. Each activity for the day's lesson should be written on the line next to the box. Feel free to use a second page, as needed. As each thing is completed during the lesson, check it off. Any areas where the student needs more work should be detailed on the "Notes" line. You should use these notes to create the next lesson plan.

Student ___Johnny Smith___   Date _____

LESSON PLAN

Each individual activity in the day's lesson should be written on its own line next to a box. As you get through each activity for the lesson, check it off. Any steps in the student's program that are now complete or any areas that need more practice should be detailed on the "Notes" line. Use those notes to create the next Lesson Plan.

☐   Review problem letters b, d, p, q _____

     Notes: _____

☐   Draw pictures that start with the b sound (balloon, ball, boy, baby, bed, bat). Repeat with d, p, q

     Notes: _____

☐   Practice writing lowercase letters _____

     Notes: _____

☐   Play games with alphabet cards _____

     Notes: _____

☐   Do next three pages from workbook _____

     Notes: _____

☐   Play games with alphabet cards _____

     Notes: _____

☐   Practice writing uppercase letters _____

     Notes: _____

Student _____   Date _____

LESSON PLAN

Each individual activity in the day's lesson should be written on its own line next to a box. As you get through each activity for the lesson, check it off. Any steps in the student's program that are now complete or any areas that need more practice should be detailed on the "Notes" line. Use those notes to create the next Lesson Plan.

☐ _____

Notes: _____

☐ _____

Notes: _____

☐ _____

Notes: _____

☐ _____

Notes: _____

☐ _____

Notes: _____

☐ _____

Notes: _____

☐ _____

Notes: _____

Notes:

And that's it, folks!

May you make great progress and have tons of fun!

If you have difficulties, questions, or feedback on any of the steps in this manual, feel free to send an email to info@ FirstStepPhonics.com. One of my staff or myself will do our best to reply in a timely manner.

If you find success with this manual, I invite you to post a review where you purchased it or submit a testimonial (and a photo or video, if possible) to info@FirstStepPhonics.com.

Thank you and best of luck!

—Veronica Blade

More from First Step Phonics

LEVEL ZERO

LEVEL ONE

More from First Step Phonics

LEVEL TWO

LEVEL THREE

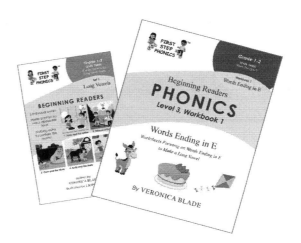

LEVEL FOUR - COMING SOON!

First Step Phonics books and workbooks start with the basics and gradually build, giving your student the tools needed to conquer every word at every level.

Level 0
Workbooks 1–3 focus on the alphabet, upper & lowercase
(3 workbooks)
Workbooks 4–6 concentrate on the sounds of the alphabet
(3 workbooks)

Level 1
Early readers that contain only short-vowel 3-letter words
(This level includes 25 reading books plus 5 workbooks)

Level 2
Early readers that build on short vowels by introducing consonant blends, like *fast, print, scrap, branch*
(This level includes 25 reading books plus 5 workbooks)

Level 3
Early readers that focus on words ending in E to make a long vowel sound, such as *mane, rope, cute, hike*
(This level includes 5 reading books plus 1 workbook)

Level 4
Early readers that utilize words with two vowels together that make one sound, such as *beep, meal, paid, cloud*
(This level contains 25 reading books plus 5 workbooks)

Go to FirstStepPhonics.com for Levels 0–4 books and workbooks. Find our YouTube channel for teaching videos, read-along book videos and more.

Veronica Blade, author of *How to Teach Anyone to Read*, lives in Gardnerville, Nevada, with her husband and furbabies. She is a best-selling romance author and also has thousands of hours experience teaching phonics over several decades. She has worked with countless students of all ages, resulting in dramatically improved reading skills. Her early-reader books and workbooks are designed utilizing a successful method which can give your student the tools to sound out words, quickly build their confidence, and increase their ability to learn other subjects.

Printed in Great Britain
by Amazon

78974178R00061